The Reset: A Divine Journey

Vini Seetharamaiah

BookLeaf Publishing

India | USA | UK

Presentation by *BookLeaf Publishing*

Web: www.bookleafpub.com

E-mail: info@bookleafpub.com

ISBN: 9789363315945

First edition 2024

*To the misfits, the dreamers, and those who feel
out of place,
This book is for you.
May it bring you hope and remind you of your
true essence,
bigger than the confines of the human self.
The universe makes no mistakes—you are
exactly who you're meant to be.
Embrace your uniqueness,
for you are perfect, just as you are!*

ACKNOWLEDGEMENT

This book would not have been possible without the love and support of many incredible individuals.

To my mum, dad, and mama, thank you for your unwavering belief in me and for always encouraging me to follow my passions. Your love has been my foundation.

To my friends, Ari, and Xen, who have been my sounding boards and cheerleaders, your support means the world to me. Thank you for listening, offering feedback, and celebrating each milestone with me.

To my spiritual guides, your wisdom and guidance have profoundly shaped my journey. Thank you for accepting me as I am, helping me see the light within and for inspiring me to share my truth.

A special thank you to BookLeaf Publishing for helping me take the first step and for your invaluable assistance in bringing this book to life.

And to all those who have supported me, whether mentioned here by name or not, please know that your kindness and encouragement have left an indelible mark on my heart.

Finally, to my readers, thank you for embarking on this journey with me. May *The Reset: A Divine Journey* inspire and guide you toward your own spiritual awakening and inner transformation.

With heartfelt gratitude,

Vini x

PREFACE

Welcome to *The Reset: A Divine Journey.* My name is Vini, and this book marks a significant milestone in my life. It's my first sonnet collection and my first book, inspired by a profound spiritual calling and my journey through what many call the "dark night of the soul," — a phase of life where every being is forced to awaken to their true nature (it's not a pretty stage but it's essential as it brings many gifts that one isn't even aware of).

The inspiration for this book came from my desire to help others break free from the conditioning that begins at birth—shaped by family, school, and society—that often leads us to live on autopilot, disconnected from our true selves. A child isn't born with insecurities or hatred; these emotions are forced upon them due to trauma inflicted by those who were meant to provide a safe space for their pure expressions. When that child grows up and chooses not to break the cycle, generations of broken children are raised, perpetuating a cycle of pain and disconnection. This disconnection from the divine is the root cause of most mental illnesses in society. My hope through these sonnets is to paint a picture of my own spiritual journey and perspective, to inspire you and reveal the beauty that lies within the spiritual path, and to encourage you to take a step towards it.

Each sonnet in this collection represents a unique spiritual stage or concept, guiding you step-by-step toward a deeper understanding of your true nature. These poems are not meant to introduce new ideas but to help your soul remember what it already knows deep within. Throughout the book, you will notice the use of "he," "she," and "they" interchangeably. These pronouns are meant to resonate with you, the reader, regardless of your gender, emphasising that these spiritual truths are universal and deeply personal.

My personal journey has taught me that the soul holds profound wisdom and that by reconnecting with our true selves, we can heal past conditioning and pave the way for future generations. This book aims to help you remember who you really are and to encourage you to embark on your own journey of healing and transformation.

To everyone who has supported me on this path, thank you. Your love and guidance have been invaluable.

As you read these sonnets, I invite you to open your heart and mind, letting your soul resonate with the beauty and truth within these words. May you find a life full of joy, purpose, and spiritual freedom with the guidance of *The Reset*.

With love and light,

Vini x

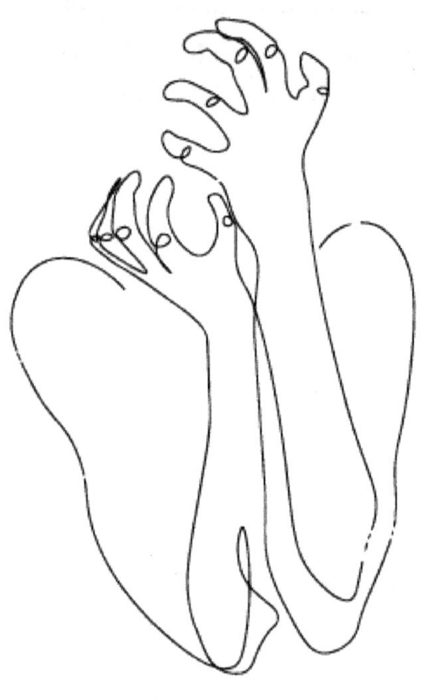

Shattered Illusions

A life once bright now dimmed by endless rules,
From early dreams to systems that confine.
In every step, the world demands its dues,
And freedom fades as chains of duty bind.

A path is walked, not chosen by the heart,
A script imposed, each line a heavy cage.
Injustice reigns, tearing the soul apart,
The world's design, a bitter, hollow stage.

All is questioned—what worth is there in breath,
When life's a play where masks must hide the
face?
Despair so deep, there's yearning just for death,
To end the pain, escape this ruthless chase.

Is life itself a lie that veils the truth,
Or is peace found only by embracing ruth?

The Awakening

In depths where shadows whisper doubt and
fear,
A soul descends to touch the darkest night.
In pain's abyss, the heart begins to clear,
For only loss reveals the hidden light.

Despair, the teacher, calls the spirit's name,
To see beyond the veil of life's façade.
In sorrow's grip, a spark ignites a flame,
A beacon in the void, the soul applauds.

From the ashes of defeat, a phoenix soars,
Awakening to truth, the heart's embrace.
In darkness found, the light within restores,
And shadows flee before the dawn's new grace.

In rock bottom's embrace, the spirit learned,
To find the light, the soul must first be burned.

Stillness

In stillness found, he meets his soul's retreat,
Where light now guides him through the silent veil.
In quiet depths, his heart begins to beat,
A rhythm echoing beyond the frail.

He ponders questions vast, of life's true worth,
Of truths once held but now like shadows fall.
In contemplation, witnesses the world's rebirth,
And feels the lies that bound his spirit's call.

The whispered doubts, the lessons taught in vain,
Dissolve like mist before the morning sun.
In stillness, wonders what is false and plain,
And seeks the truth beneath what's said and done.

He realises that the mind's illusions do deceive,
In silence, finds the courage to believe.

Self-Discovery

In silent depths, she starts to see within,
A soul encased in layers thick and tight.
The roles imposed by world's relentless spin,
Conceal her truth, obscure her inner light.

She sees the masks, the facades crafted well,
By expectations, norms, and rigid rules.
A stranger in a story she can't tell,
Lost in a maze of others' chosen tools.

Yet in the stillness, clarity unfolds,
Revealing truths beneath the layers' weight.
The falsehoods shed, her spirit now beholds,
A path unmasked, a chance to recreate.

With courage born of introspective quest,
She strips away, to find her truest self expressed.

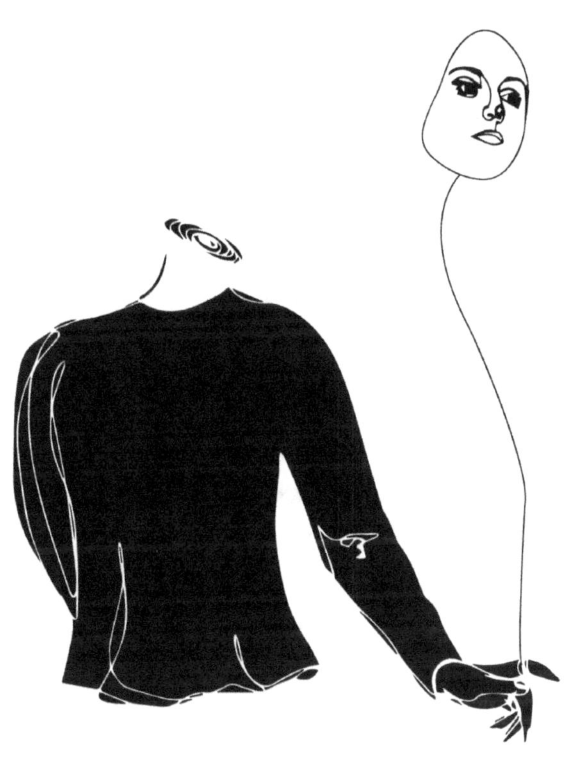

The inner child

In meditative silence, deep and true,
A voice emerges, soft, yet full of light.
The inner child, forgotten but not through,
Awakens now within his soul's pure sight.

Tears stream as memories flood his mind,
Of years when innocence was cast aside.
The child, with eyes so wise, so kind,
Embraces all the pain he sought to hide.

"Forgive me," whispers flow from soul to soul,
For all the times the child was left alone.
But joy now fills the space that once was cold,
The child's delight, a warmth that's newly
grown.

In unity, they merge, the healing done,
The child within now shines, his spirit one.

Meditation

In mindful depths, she ventures further still,
Exploring realms within her quiet mind.
A journey marked by courage, strength, and
will,
To seek the self that she was meant to find.

She walks the path through memories and
dreams,
Through shadows cast by doubts and fleeting
fears.
In silence, golden light within her beams,
A soul that shines through all her darkest years.

The soul, aglow with wisdom pure and bright,
Embraces her for all her leaps of faith.
It whispers truths that guide her to the light,
Unveiling origins, her path, and wraith.

In mindful peace, she learns to truly see;
Her golden soul reveals her truest "me."

Harmony with nature

With newfound wisdom, he begins his walk,
Each step a marvel, like the very first.
The earth beneath him feels alive and talks,
With whispers of the soul, a sacred burst.

Among the trees, he feels their ancient grace,
Their roots entwined with his, a bond so deep.
The leaves caress his skin, a soft embrace,
As if his soul and nature's secrets keep.

The flowers' colours bloom within his sight,
Their petals sing a song of pure delight.
He sees the beauty in each living light,
Their souls aglow, reflecting his insight.

In every creature, plant, and tree, he finds,
A mirrored truth, connection of all kinds.

Sacred Rituals

Enchanted by the bond with nature's heart,
She yearns to delve into the spirit's call.
To sacred rituals, she's drawn to start,
In search of truths that light and life enthral.

She seeks the rites once scorned by sceptic
minds,
The ancient ways that whisper to her soul.
Through chants and dances, deeper truths she
finds,
A journey that will make her spirit whole.

With open heart, she steps into the flame,
The sacred circle where the old ways shine.
Through rituals, she sheds her past and shame,
Awakens to the magic of her divine.

In sacred rites, her soul begins to soar,
Discovering truths that light her being's core.

The Astral

He ventures now where subtle planes reside,
A realm unseen by eyes, but felt within.
A world where spirits of the past abide,
An astral plane where soul's true quests begin.

With senses heightened, he perceives the veil,
That separates the physical from the soul.
In this ethereal world, where dreams prevail,
He feels the presence of a truth untold.

Unbound by laws of physics, he can soar,
Through timeless space where purest visions
bloom.
His spirit free, he opens every door,
Exploring realms beyond the earthly gloom.

In astral planes, his soul begins to see,
The boundless depths of his eternity.

Ancestral Wisdom

In astral planes, profound insights arise,
Revelations once hidden now unfold.
Illusions fade, and truth before her lies,
A wisdom ancient, deep, and pure as gold.

She meets her ancestors, spirits grand,
Who walked the earth with grace and esoteric
lore.
Their presence strong, they gently take her hand,
Instilling truths that time has long ignored.

They speak of realms beyond the human mind,
Of secrets held before the world began.
Their words, like light, leave shadows far
behind,
And in their glow, she glimpses her greater plan.

Moved by the wisdom, tears begin to flow,
As ancient truths within her spirit grow.

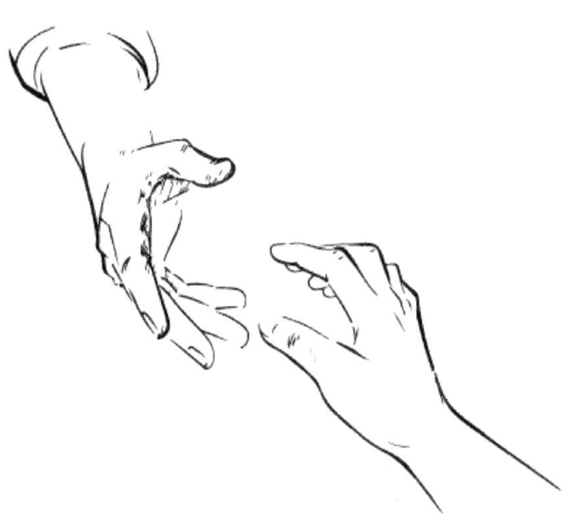

Spirit Team

In realms beyond, he finds a love so pure,
A presence felt, yet often left unseen.
These beings guide with hearts that reassure,
Their love transcends what human minds can
glean.

They walk beside him, though he's unaware,
In every step, they offer silent aid.
Their gentle whispers drift through the air,
A spirit team in whom his trust is laid.

Unseen, they celebrate each small step he takes,
Rejoicing in his growth and triumphs bright.
They share his grief, the sorrow his heart breaks,
With love that comforts in the darkest night.

They ask for nothing, yet their love is true,
These spirit guides, his soul's own loyal crew.

Synchronicities

She wakes to find her spirit team's embrace,
A constant presence since her earthly birth.
Their guiding light has set her steady pace,
With synchronicities that prove their worth.

In angel numbers, signs that catch her eye,
In thoughts of friends who call her right away,
In answers found where questions lingered high,
In phrases echoed, guiding through the day.

She sees their hand in every subtle nudge,
In every timely answer, sign, and clue.
Their love and wisdom in her life's each budge,
A dance of fate that leads her to what's true.

Awakened now, she feels their tender care;
Her spirit team has always been right there.

Dreams & Visions

His dreams now bloom with vivid, vibrant hues,
As spiritual progress opens gates.
In visions clear, his path ahead he views,
With symbols packed with wisdom that elates.

His past pains rise, yet healing they invite,
Transformed by guidance from his spirit's kin.
Through dreams, his soul reclaims its lost
birthright,
Revealing truths that dwell in depths within.

His spirit guides, in shadows, weave their light,
With ancestors who whisper through the night.
In dreams, he finds the key to his true might,
His purpose clear, his role now in his sight.

Each vision, rich with meaning, leads the way,
To heal, transform, and shine a brighter day.

Past Life Reflections

In dreams, her past lives come to vivid light,
She sees the realms and planets where she's
been.
In vibrant hues, the energies ignite,
A tapestry of love, war, and peace within.

She feels the joy and sorrow once endured,
The echoes of her soul's long journey told.
Through visions clear, her essence is assured,
The reasons for her existence now unfold.

She sees the karmic threads that weave her fate,
The duties bound by choices of the past.
Profound insights on gifts she must create,
The wisdoms earned through lifetimes, made to
last.

In this grand tapestry, her soul's design,
She finds the truths that make her spirit shine.

Soul Contracts

In visions clear, he sees the souls once met,
Across the span of lifetimes, past and now.
Each encounter crafted by a debt,
Of contracts signed with a sacred, silent vow.

He understands the ties that bind him here,
The reasons for each friendship and each foe.
Through joy or strife, the lessons are crystal
clear,
In love and pain, his soul begins to grow.

No meeting by chance, no bond without a cause,
Each played a role in life's grand, staged ballet.
A dance of spirits, bound by cosmic laws,
Each step a lesson, paving wisdom's way.

He sees the truth behind life's grand illusion,
In every heart, a piece of his inclusion.

Shadow Work

With newfound strength, she turns to face the
shade,
The shadow self she once had feared to see.
No longer will she let the darkness fade,
But integrate it, setting her soul free.

The self she hid to conform and belong,
To meet the norms society had cast,
Now emerges as a strength to make her spirit
strong,
She greets the shadows, healing from the past.

In darkness, she finds gifts long kept at bay,
A yin and yang that balance, whole, and true.
She sees the power in the night and day,
The light within the shadow's deeper hue.

Embracing all, she stands as one, complete,
A soul now potent, grounded, and replete.

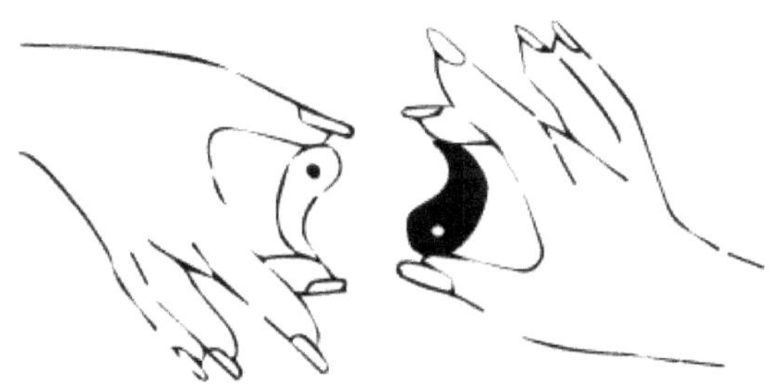

Seven Chakras

He tunes into the forces deep within,
The vibrant centres where his energies flow.
Each chakra spins, sparks of light begin,
In hues that make his inner essence glow.

From root to crown, the colours intertwine,
A spectrum so bright within his sacred core.
Red grounds his being, orange passions find,
With yellow's power, green's love, he restores.

Blue speaks his truth, indigo's insight guides,
And violet's spirit lifts him to the skies.
Each centre's balance, where his soul abides,
Aligns his life with joy and makes him wise.

In harmony, his chakras' light does gleam,
Evolving the soul in life's eternal stream.

Kundalini Rising

She now perceives within each human soul,
Two energies that lie in dormant rest.
Divine feminine, masculine make whole,
Twin serpents coiled, awaiting their quest.

At soul's deep root, these forces gently lie,
The feminine's grace, the masculine's might.
When roused, they rise together, reaching high,
Unleashing the soul's power, pure and infinite.

Their union brings a bliss beyond compare,
A sacred flow that's felt in every vein.
An ecstasy that's not of worldly fare,
But cosmic joy, divine and free of strain.

Kundalini's rise, a god-like birth,
Becoming one with all—the soul and the earth.

Universal Energies

He now perceives the energies divine,
That flow through every being, boundless, free.
A power from the source, pure and benign,
In galaxies, in stars, in you and me.

This force, called God, or Spirit, Universe,
Imbues the sun, the planets, earth, and skies.
In nature's pulse, its presence does immerse,
In human hearts, it silently abides.

The names may differ, yet the essence one,
A universal power, vast and grand.
It fuels all life, from dawn till day is done,
An endless stream from love's eternal hand.

He feels this force within him, bright and strong,
A timeless energy where all belong.

Unity & Oneness

She sees beyond the veil of false divide,
And knows the truth that lies in every breath.
The illusion of separation now denied,
She is the universe in life and in death.

She is the stars, the galaxies' grand dance,
The very subtle force that binds it all.
In every element, she finds her stance,
In air and fire, in water's rise and fall.

She is the earth, the mountains, and the sea,
The whispering winds, the sunlight's warm
embrace.
She is the nature, whole and wild and free,
She is the cosmos, infinite in space.

In this profound and cosmic unity,
She finds her soul's eternal harmony.

Transcendence

He transcends now, to realms of joy and bliss,
A state of purest love, so serene and bright.
Beyond the fleeting lure of earthly kiss,
He finds the truth in the inner, sacred light.

No longer bound by the material ties,
He soars where joy and beauty know no end.
In endless peace, his spirit gently flies,
With love that all of reality does transcend.

This state, beyond the pleasures of the flesh,
Reveals the purpose humans seek and yearn.
To rise above the physical and mesh,
With inner power, where true beauties burn.

This is the point, the path of evolution,
To find within, the soul's own revolution.

The Reset

42

Dear reader, listen to the yearning in your heart,
A call from deep within your soul's own plea.
To nurture, heal, and from old ways depart,
To find the light that sets your spirit free.

Your soul desires to guide you to this state,
Where joy and love transcend all earthly gain.
Release the past, the fears that dominate,
And cleanse your mind from falsehoods that
remain.

Begin anew, with fresh and open eyes,
Embrace the path your inner self will set.
Let go of all the worldly, fleeting ties,
Embark upon this journey with no regret.

Answer the call, your true self you beget,
And start anew, embrace the great reset!